Feeding the Hungry in the First World
A Step-By-Step Guide For Starting or Revamping a Food Pantry and/or Soup Kitchen in the United States

By Amber Wood Sellars

Contents:

I0117119

Hello. My name is Amber. I am 27 years old and I live in a First World country called The United States of America. There are hungry people where I live. "Whaaaaat?" you ask? "Hungry people in the US? That's crazy talk. You mean like the homeless people wandering the streets of Chicago and New York City, right?" No. I mean like in your small wealthy town in Kentucky, California, and Connecticut. Guys, I cannot tell you how many people have looked at me dumbfounded when I have told them how many hungry people are in their communities. "We don't have hungry people here in my town." "Oh, you don't? Well statistics show otherwise; in your little 'town' of 29,000, there are 5,200 people (18%) living below the poverty line at risk for hunger. People who are having to make daily decisions like this: 'Do I use what little money I have to pay for gas today or to pay my water bill or to buy food for my family?'" It's here, guys. In our neck of the woods. Our neighbors are hungry. Are they starving and dying of malnutrition? No. (In rare cases, yes). Are there commercials with barefoot, dirty children begging on the streets? No. In the US, we prefer to hide our inadequacies. Sure, we show thousands of commercials a minute all over the US about poor little puppies and kitties who need your "one dollar a day" which will keep them alive. I'm sick of those daggum commercials! Now, don't get me wrong, I like puppies and kitties, too. Don't put this book down just because I made a jab at puppy commercials. But, guys. Seriously. Where are the commercials about the family that is living with no electricity, no heat, no water, no car, clothes that don't fit, and three cans of vegetables in their cabinets? People with "full-time jobs" who still cannot provide the basic needs for their family. Those people exist. In the hundreds of thousands. In *our* country. In *your* community. In *your* backyard. The most recent statistics tally the numbers to 46 million Americans (16% of our entire population) living under the poverty line, at risk for hunger. 46 million. *46 million. **46 MILLION.*** Here. Not in Africa, not in South America, not in some country we can't pronounce. HERE. I'm all for efforts to address poverty and hunger all over the world, friends. My husband and I donate to a multitude of causes addressing just that. But we all forget about one spot on the map that needs help! THE UNITED STATES OF AMERICA. If you don't have the money to send overseas, if you don't have the time or resources to get on a plane and bring food to the needy in Africa, I get it. I understand. *However*, you ***don't*** have an excuse to not help in your own TOWN or CITY! Let's fix this problem. I'm ashamed, astonished, and amazed at the hunger epidemic in the "Land of the Free and Home of the Brave". Let's tackle it. Let's abolish it. We all have a responsibility to level the playing field for everybody in our nation. We want kids to excel in school and be the leaders of tomorrow? That's hard to do when you haven't eaten in two days and you can't think of anything else but lunchtime. We want people in our workforce to be respectable contributors to society? That's hard to do when you gave all of the food you had to your children so they could eat while you went hungry. I'm fed up with hunger. Let's kick hunger's ass. Together. The time is now. Here we go.

Where to Begin

Okay, so you want to start a food pantry and/or a soup kitchen, huh? If you're reading this, I'm going to guess that that answer is yes. I'm also going to guess that you care about people, you're tired of living in a first world country where people are struggling to put food on their tables for their families, and you have a passion for justice, right? Me too. That's why I've devoted my life to feeding those in need and teaching others (*you*) how to do the same. Before you read any further though, I must ask you this: Do you truly have a passion for change? Do you have time, energy, and emotion to commit to this? If the answer is no to either question, put this book down or hand it to someone else. Starting and maintaining a *successful* food pantry and/or soup kitchen takes dedication, it takes work, it takes constant vigor, and the willingness to do a little head banging and losing a little hair and a little sleep along the way. Are you still reading? If you are, then you are somebody I want to meet and befriend! You are just the kind of person I want to high five and give a little friendly punch in the shoulder and say "Let's make people's lives better!" to. Thank you for being generally awesome. Alrighty, now that that's out of the way, let's dive in, shall we?

Part I: Getting A Non-Profit Status

Unless you are a multi-millionaire and you want to spend your personal money making this thing work, you will need to get yourself set up as a Non-Profit Charity. If you *are* a multi-millionaire and want to spend your personal money supporting a food pantry, please call me. If you aren't, you need to do a few crucial steps to get started – the first being getting your Non-Profit Status (in the IRS world, this is called a 501(c)(3); why can't they just call it "Charity"? I don't know either). Now, this can take awhile. For my first one, it took 9 months. The second took 5 months. Depending on how "busy" the IRS is, it could take anywhere from 3-18 months. But I want to start *now*, you say? You can! You just can't give donors "tax-deductible receipts" until you get that status. But you can still operate. So, go ahead and put in the legwork while you're waiting to hear back from the IRS so that once you get your status, you are ready to run! There are several steps involved in getting your status:

1. Pick a Name. This is fun, right? You get to name your nonprofit whatever you want. Well, almost. Make sure to follow these rules:

> - The name cannot be the same as the name of any other corporation on file with the state's corporations division.
> - About half of all states require the name to end with a corporate designator, such as Corporation (Corp.), Incorporated (Inc. – most likely what you'll want to choose) or Limited (Ltd.).
> - Your name cannot contain certain designations reserved for the state, such as United States, Reserve, Federal, National, Cooperative or Bank.

2. File Articles of Incorporation (find the form for your state online) with your state. This just means that you tell the state that you are officially establishing a nonprofit organization. Contact your state's attorney general or secretary's office to obtain the necessary paperwork (easiest to do online). Some states require a small fee, so be prepared to send a $10-$50 dollar check with your paperwork. You will have to provide the names of your *Board of Directors* in this application. Who should your Board be comprised of? Anybody who is willing to join in your efforts to feed people. My first one consisted of my grandfather, a minister, myself, my co-director, and a community member. There's no magical combination or requirements for the Board of Directors; they just need to be on board (no pun intended, but I'm quite witty) with what you're doing. You will meet with these people once a month (ish) to talk about how things are going and to make decisions on new things to try. If you can get financial "big wigs" who are willing to open their wallets for your cause to be on your Board…even better. Are you feeling overwhelmed already with weird names (501(c)(3) and "Board of Directors")? Don't. I have been doing this for a while and when I started, I had NO idea what I was doing! I still fly by the seat of my pants at times (shhh). These names and rules are just formalities necessary to do this thing well and correctly. Hang in there with me as we get through this IRS part.

So, what will happen is: You will send your Articles of Incorporation to your state. You will wait for the Secretary of State (or his/her personal name stamper) to stamp your form and send it back to you. Once you get this valuable piece of paper back with that special stamp, you will be considered an "incorporated organization". How cool, right? You're incorporated. It made me feel fancy. Then, you will send your stamped Articles of Incorporation to the IRS along with all of the other application parts you need to make the IRS happy (the main form is called "Form 1023"; there is also a supplemental form called "Form SS-4"). While you are waiting for the Articles of Incorporation to come back, you should work on filling out your *Form 1023* (found online at irs.gov) and SS-4.

3. **File SS-4 (EIN: Employer Identification Number).** Regardless of whether or not you have employees, nonprofits are required to obtain a federal Employer Identification Number (EIN), which is also referred to as the federal ID number. This number is used to identify your organization when tax documents are filed and is used not unlike an individual's Social Security number. This little special number will be what you use on all of your tax-deductible receipts that you give people who donate money to you. You will also use it on all kinds of paperwork.

4. **Create a Mission Statement, Budget, and Bylaws.** These are things you will need to submit with your big IRS Form 1023 paperwork.
    a. **Mission Statement:** The mission statement is a concise expression that covers in 1 or 2 sentences the name of the organization, what it does, for whom it performs services, and where it dispenses services. It should also portray how your organization is different from others like it. Make your mission statement compelling. You want people to read it and want to contribute to your cause! You will use your mission statement in brochures, flyers, your website (if you choose to create one), etc. Here is an example: "The mission of Harvesting Hope Food Pantry, Inc. is to reduce the amount of hunger in Boyle County through community cooperation, making the best possible use of all available resources."

b. **Budget:** You may have no idea what your budget is going to look like or should look like. That's ok. For right now, the IRS just wants to see what you *anticipate* your budget to be for the next two years. No big deal if you end up being WAY off!

c. **Bylaws**: The bylaws are just the rules your organization is going to go by. Look in the forms section for an example. Again, these are up to you and you won't be quizzed on them or expected to make them beautifully written in legalese (jargon). These aren't always necessary to submit with your Form 1023, but you will need them afterwards, so it's best to just go ahead and do them.

5. **Sumbit IRS Form 1023.** Okay, now that you've got all of your pieces, you can send your Form 1023 with your EIN written on it and your budget, mission statement, and bylaws attached to it to the IRS. You will have to submit $850 (unless the fee changes) with your application. Once it has been sent, it's just another waiting game. You can always ask them to expedite it. I put a sample of this form in the forms section also. If you have an attorney friend or friend of a friend, see if they will give things a look for you before you send everything. It's always nice to have someone who knows what they're doing looking at your "baby".

6. **File for state and local tax exemption.** Once you've gotten your "Letter of Determination" (the IRS 501c3 letter you get after filing your Form 1023; the big daddy that allows you to get donations and give people tax-deductible receipts) for tax exemption at the federal level, you can also apply for tax exemption for state and local taxes. This is awesome because you don't have to pay sales tax when you go to Walmart or Lowes or Home Depot or really, when you pay almost any bill! Every little bit of money saved helps! You can find the forms you need online.

7. **Feed People!** Okay, you've done all of the grunge work and you've played the waiting game, now it's time to get donations and feed people. The next chapter will talk all about ways to go about getting funding for your valiant project.

Money

Alright, you know the sayings "Money makes the world go 'round" and "It takes money to make money"? Well, as it turns out, they are both true. Even for nonprofits. Before I started all of this, my thought was "hey, it can't take all that much money to feed people, can it?" Well, I was so off the mark. It takes a **lot** of money to feed people. Why? Because feeding people *successfully* requires not just food and a big heart, but a building, staff, supplies, utilities, cars, gas, and all kinds of other miscellaneous expenses. We'll talk more about that in the "Building Expenses" chapter, but for now, our focus is going to be on how to *get* money, not ways you're going to have to painstakingly *spend* it. So, let's start with businesses.

1. **Businesses**: The best way to get a food pantry and/or soup kitchen started and productively maintained is to get one or two generous businesses to back you. If you can get a few businesses to financially support your overhead (i.e. utilities, staff payroll, building rent, gas), then all of the money you get from donors can be spent on the biggest expense: food. How do I get businesses to back us? Easy. **Use your connections!** Find a family member or friend who owns a business or knows somebody who owns a business and tackle that angle. Remind any business you talk to that their contributions are tax-deductible so it will benefit them. Negotiate with them and let them know that you will promote their business and let your community know that they are generously involved with your effort to feed your community. It may lead to them generating more business simply because their name is attached to your charitable efforts. Decide what your overhead costs are going to be – including building rent/mortgage, staff payroll, utilities, supplies, maintenance, uniforms, printing, brochures, etc. – and ask the business(es) to donate that amount of money each month. If you can snag these monies, then your main focus and most important focus can be on generating donations for food.
2. **Donors**: Don't count out other businesses as donor sources once you snag your one or two big business contributors.

Talk to every business in your community and ask them to donate as well. Share with them the same benefits you shared with the large business donors. Beyond the businesses in your community, talk with churches, boy scout groups, school groups, families, and individuals. Donors and your relationship with them are *so incredibly* important. Use whatever means necessary to get them and keep them. Make donating easy for anybody to do. Develop a way for people to donate online, through the mail, via phone. Put up a billboard in your community that tells people how to donate. Send out mass mailings (the post office can help with this) to encourage people to donate. Post information about your organization and how to donate in your local newspaper, tv stations, radio stations. When you get a donation, make sure you have a good record system (preferably on the computer instead of pen and paper; I use littlegreenlight.com) to track it and then send that donor a thank you letter. Constantly update your donors about things going on in your organization – how many people you've fed that month, what their money has done for people in need, how many families are being served because of their donations, etc. I have included samples of thank you letters and stats sheets in the Forms section. Send your donors brochures and magnets to remind them what their money is going towards.

3. **Grants**: You can never apply for too many grants! From my experience, grants for food pantries are pretty hard to come by, but don't give up. If you feel like "whaaaat? writing a grant?! I have no idea how to write a grant", that's okay. There are plenty of websites with tips and teaching tools in regards to grant writing. There are also plenty of websites with information about all of the grants in your area. I have also included a sample in the Forms section.

4. **Fundraisers**: Like grants, you can never do too many fundraisers! Sell t-shirts, organize a golf scramble, sit outside of Wal-Mart and do a bake sale or simply ask for donations, organize a car wash. See if you can get businesses to donate items to auction off. Do a karaoke night with a cover charge. No idea is silly when you are trying to raise money to feed hungry people.

Staff

Boy oh boy, is this chapter important. There are so many facets that go into creating a good, solid, hard-working, dedicated, fun staff. First, I'll give you the list of staff you will need and their job descriptions and then I will give you some things to think about before you start gathering people to join you in taking care of your "baby".

Staff Positions:

Executive Director: This is what my role is in the two non-profit organizations I run. I recommend giving this position away so you don't have to do it haha Only kidding (a little). This is the most important position and it comes with the most responsibilities and the most headaches. You are the head honcho, the captain of the ship, the leader of the ranks, the hero when things go right and the scapegoat when things go wrong (and let me assure you, things *will* go wrong sometimes!). Whoever assumes this role is in charge of keeping track of donors, keeping track of (and paying!) bills, accounting, payroll, filing taxes, keeping up with all statistics and paperwork, making and maintaining relationships with donors, networking for resources, staying on top of *all* daily tasks of all other staff members, answering an ungodly amount of phone calls and emails, fixing anything that breaks or goes wrong, keeping up staff and volunteer morale, keeping the pantry stocked with food and supplies, and on and on and on with any other minute details that fill each day. The Executive Director is the face of the organization. If you take this roll, you will be expected to be involved in community events, to speak at various locations about what you're all about, and to be a familiar face in your community. It's a fun job and most of the time it's just rewarding and a blast to be, but there are times you will want to just run away and hide under a rock because of all the crazy things that can happen when you're in charge! There is no one else above you to point blame at or to ask for help. It's on your shoulders, so start lifting weights now to get ready ☺

Co-Director: Now, you don't necessarily "need" a co-director, but boy are you going to want one! I didn't have one when I started and I *quickly* realized that was a mistake! Re-read that above job description for the Executive Director. The Co-Director's job is to help the Executive Director with anything and everything. Share the responsibilities. Share the triumphs and share the disasters. Personally, I could not function without my co-director.

Pantry Manager: Okay, this is the real backbone of your operation. The pantry manager is a full-time staff member who's job is to be present every second the pantry is open (and before and after a lot of the time!). This person's job description is similar to the Executive Director's in terms of the scope of tasks; the pantry manager will manage everything going on *inside* the pantry, while you are managing everything that is going on *outside* the pantry (behind the scenes). He/she will manage volunteers, make sure she (I'm just going to say "she" from here on out because our amazing pantry manager is indeed a woman) knows who is coming to help out each day, stock food, organize food, sign people in, keep track of records, talk with people who come in to learn about our organization, keep track of food donations brought in by donors, organize the volunteer efforts – from shopping with people to cleaning bathrooms – she will be the first one in and the last one out, in charge of opening up and locking up, she will be the friendly face each "patron" sees and gets to know, she will be the one calling you when there is a problem ("we ran out of toilet paper!", "our food delivery truck is 2 hours late!", "there's a guy in here causing trouble", "the potatoes rotted and need to be thrown out", "the cooler is broken!" etc. etc. etc.). You cannot function without the pantry manager. Make sure you have people on board with you who will "fill in" for the pantry manager if she's sick or on vacation!

Volunteer Coordinator: This person is responsible for recruiting and keeping up with volunteers. This person should write "thank you" letters to volunteers, interview volunteers before they come in and start working, calling or emailing volunteers to remind them about their scheduled time, etc.

Food Coordinator: This person will keep up with the amount and kinds of foods in the pantry. When certain items get low, this person will order the food online or in stores and either pick it up or have it delivered. This person will need to coordinate closely with the pantry manager because the pantry manager is in the pantry everyday and will know exactly what is needed and when.

Cook: If you are going to include a soup kitchen with your feeding the hungry efforts, you are going to need a cook. Ours is phenomenal! She is kind and energetic and loves what she does. The cook does not need to be a full-time employee. Ours usually comes in in the mornings and prepares the meal(s) for the day and then leaves. The pantry manager is there to oversee that everything runs smoothly in the soup kitchen. (*Sidenote: We separate our food pantry times and our soup kitchen times so it isn't a "cluster _____" of chaos and craziness. Our food pantry hours are in the morning and afternoon, and our soup kitchen hours are in the evening).

Paid Volunteer: We also pay a volunteer a minimal amount each month to be there everyday to help our pantry manager. This person is not an "employee", but you still pay this person monthly (or weekly or however works best for you) to help and be available.

Food Pick-Uper (classy name, right?): We pay a guy to drive all over town every day to pick up food from the restaurants and other establishments that donate food to us daily. Hopefully if you network well, you will need one of these guys, too! (We'll talk about that in a different chapter).

Now, you can create whatever kind of staff you want. You don't have to have *your* Executive Director do everything that I do. And you could have your pantry manager be in charge of volunteers and your Co-Director in charge of food orders. That's all up to you. This is just how it happens to work for us. Depending on how many people you will be trying to feed each month, your needs will change. We feed an average of 2,000 people every month. Your organization may be bigger or smaller and thus your staff needs will be different.

What the heck do I pay my staff, you ask? Good question. That is going to depend on what kind of money you are bringing in. If you have gotten two businesses to agree to pay for your overhead, whatever set amount they are willing to pay is what you need to look at and break down in order to figure out how much money you will have available to you after paying utilities, rent, etc. to pay your staff. In the beginning, your staff may have to be comfortable with playing the pay game by ear. Figure out what you will be able to pay initially, and then increase that to the amount you desire as time goes on.

Make sure your staff all get along and like each other! This isn't an office building where you are all sitting at computers and working on menial tasks all day long. You will all be up and moving and working to feed hungry people and love people and make a difference in your community. You want to be around people who think like you do, care like you do, and want to make a difference in a fun way like you do! Be sure to do things together that promote camaraderie and fun. We do bowling outings and any type of get together that involves food to keep our spirits up and to check in and make sure everybody is doing okay and still doing what they love and loving what they do.

Volunteers

Me: Okay, remember how I said the chapter about staff was really important?

You: Yes, Amber, that was the last chapter before this one. I *just* read it. Thank you for trusting in my ability to remember something for 5 seconds. Hint: That was sarcasm.

Me: Noted. Well, this chapter is probably even more important than that one.

You: I'm listening….

Me: Good. Because if you skip this chapter, your food pantry will *fail*. Fail hard.

Got your attention? Good. Hear me when I say this: Your volunteers will **make or break** your organization. You *need* them. Treat them like Kings and Queens. Geez, even address them as Kings and Queens! "Good morning, Queen Volunteer Jane" (respectful, reverent bow inserted here). I'm serious. If you can be fortunate enough to create a solid, committed, energetic, reliable, servant-minded volunteer group…you will have the best organization in the universe. You may be amazing. Heck, I think I'm pretty fantastic most of the time (I pray for humility a *lot* because cockiness and conceitedness come way too easily and naturally for me), but I *know* that even *I* don't have the ability to do 20 different jobs at once. You need volunteers. You needs *lots* of volunteers. Picture this: A typical day for us consists of helping anywhere between 20-50 families shop for groceries between 9:30am and 1:00pm. That's 4 hours to get all of those families taken care of, all of those families checked in, all of those families shopped, all of those families' cars loaded, while also keeping the shelves stocked, cleaning up, answering who knows how many questions and phone calls, etc. Do you want to do all of that alone? Neither does the pantry manager! And even if she *did* want to, it is humanly impossible (yes, even for you and me – the two most fabulously capable humans on the planet). So, bottom line: recruit volunteers, be kind to volunteers, praise volunteers, make volunteers' experiences fun and rewarding in any way you can.

One of the things that we do to make our volunteers feel special and like a part of our team is providing them with t-shirts. We all wear the same color t-shirt with our logo so we all feel like we're part of the same team and so shoppers and community members can recognize us. You can also sell t-shirts to make a little extra money for your pantry. We've done that, too!

Networking and Community Relationships

We are successful at what we do for a number of reasons. One big contributing factor to our success is our relationships with influential community members and businesses. I am going to let you in on an insider secret: There are so many untapped resources in your community. They are definitely out there. And they are untapped. And they are waiting for *you* to claim them! For......FREE. I'm going to share with you a few things that we do that has made our food pantry function so much better and at a lower cost!

Restaurants

In the forms section of this book, I have included a sample of a "Food Liability Waiver". Restaurants throw out *SO* much good food *EVERYDAY*. They throw it out because they don't know what else to do with it. They throw it out because they are afraid to donate it due to liability reasons. You take away the fear of liability, you can get any restaurant to donate their leftover food to you. There is a *federal* act called the "Emerson Good Samaritan Food Donation Act" enacted October 1, 1996 which was created to encourage food donation to nonprofits by minimizing liability. Each state has its own version of this act located somewhere in their statutes. For Kentucky, it's Kentucky Revised Statute 413.248; it eliminates liability to those who donate apparently wholesome food to a nonprofit organization for distribution to the needy. This means that the local friend chicken place in your community that throws out nearly *60 cooked chickens* every day at close can donate those chickens to *YOU*. We go around to various restaurants in our community, bring the food back to our pantry and serve it in our soup kitchen or bag it up in individual bags and give it out with other groceries at our food pantry. This is a *huge* resource base. Use it!

Hospitals

What is something that all hospitals have in common? They all have a cafeteria. Talk with the manager of your local hospital(s) and ask them if they will donate any leftover food they have to your organization.

Catering Companies

Have you ever been to a party that was catered and you're like "Dang! What are they going to do with all of this leftover food? Let *me* take it home! Especially those little pepperoni sandwich thingies…mmm." I totally have. Well, oftentimes the catering companies have no idea what to do with their leftovers. Give them an idea. Whisper it in their ear while they are sleeping at night, "Doooonaaaate yoooouuur leftooooooverrrs to the foooood paaaaantry…" Okay, yeah. That would be a little creepy. Go talk to them. It helps them out and makes them feel like they are contributing and it provides your pantry with more amazing food to give away to hungry people!

Grocery Stores

Oh man. This one is a biggie. Here's something a lot of people don't know about grocery stores. If they have cans that are dented, cereal boxes that have dings, bags that are incorrectly marked…*they cannot put them on their shelves*. So….*drumroll please* they throw them away. *aggravated scream* Make them stop! Have your local grocery store(s) call you and let you know when they have a surplus of items they cannot sell. Go pick them up. What's wrong with the green beans inside a dented green bean can? Right. Nothing. Give that can to someone who needs it! Sidenote about grocery stores: We get all of our plastic bags that we use for our shoppers from grocery stores. They have plenty to give away!

Other Businesses

Plenty of businesses have birthday parties for staff, catered lunches, pizza parties, etc. Give them a place to donate the leftovers from all of that. I can't tell you how many times we have gotten a bunch of 12-foot sandwiches from businesses who had lunch catered and couldn't quite finish all 60 feet of the sandwiches provided. That is perfectly good, clean, healthy food you can serve at your soup kitchen or give out at your pantry!

Take away point: Think outside the box. There are so many ways to tap into resources in your community. Everybody eats. Everybody. Make our food stretch!

Where and How to Buy Food

I guess this is a chapter I could have included closer to the beginning since it is the crux of your operation! Sometimes I get ahead of myself if you haven't noticed. Sorry. Okay, food. Your *food* pantry needs food in it for it to be what you're saying it is. Here's what we do to get our food:

Feeding America Hub:

In most areas, there will be an affiliate of Feeding America. It will likely be a very large warehouse and they will probably serve multiple counties' food pantries in your region. We purchase the majority of our food from such a warehouse. We can do it all online with them and schedule them to drop it off in their semi-trucks at our pantry. (That's another thing you're going to want to think about when you pick a building location; you want to have a building that can accommodate parking and also the delivery trucks that will be coming through). This is the easiest way to come by your food for your pantry.

Grocery Stores

Another thing you can do is work with a local grocery store and have them order your food in wholesale bulk for you. They have all of the connections, you just have them use them for *you* instead of for them. You pay them. They purchase the food you need. You pick it up from them and bring it to your pantry. We also do this a lot.

Local Farmers

Tap into this resource! This is the best way to get fresh produce. Farmers often have excess crops and they don't want it to go to waste. Give them a place to bring it! Local farmers also are a GREAT source for meat. See if you can work something out with a local butcher to provide meat at a reduced cost (of free) to your pantry.

Food Drives

When you suggest to your community that any group could put together a food drive for you, be prepared for all shapes and sizes of food drives throughout the year. This is a *great* way to get people both interested in what you are doing and helping your organization in a very practical way. Schools are way into doing food drives. So are churches. Tap into this resource. Encourage groups to make the food drive fun and competitive: "The classroom that brings in the most food gets a pizza party at the end of the month" or something like that. It motivates people and really makes the turnout great.

Building Expenses

Even if you can find someone to donate a building to you, you will still have plenty of building expenses you need to plan for and expect. Though I would encourage you to find a way to get a building donated to you or use one that you or someone else in your organization already owns! Leasing building space is so expensive. If you can find a building big enough to house your food pantry **and** a kitchen space, that is ideal. That's how we did it. We use an old deli and we use half of the old dining space for our food pantry and the other half for our soup kitchen seating.

Rent

Rent can be an outrageous cost. Do your best to work out a good contract with anybody willing to lease a building to you. Look into getting the building donated if at all possible. Either way, plan your budget to include rent and see if you can get your rent taken care of by a business or another generous donor. It will make your life so much happier.

Utilities

Plan on having variance in your utility cost each month. Just like at your home, in the wintertime, your bills are going to be much higher. Plan for that! Remember that you will be covering at least: water, electricity, trash (you will need large dumpsters for all of the trash you accumulate!), gas (maybe), internet (if you provide it).

Maintenance

At least once a month, there is some kind of maintenance issue that comes up in the pantry or kitchen. We need a plumber, we need an electrician, we need a heating & cooling expert, we need our tile floors professionally buffed, we need new tires for our box truck (try to get a box truck donated to you or find an old one for cheap!!), etc. Plan for unexpected maintenance expenses and, more importantly, have a list of reliable contacts for maintenance issues on hand at your pantry for when things come up.

Statistics to Keep

If you are going to "sell" your product – in this case, "we are trying to feed hungry people in our community" – you need numbers. You want to be able to accurately say, "If you donate $10, we can provide 45 meals to a person in need" or "In February we fed 1,237 people". Like I mentioned in the "Donor" section of the "Money" Chapter, people want to know where their money is going and what their money is doing. The only way for you to be able to provide that information to them is to keep good stats. I have included a few forms in the Forms section for you to look at. Do it in whatever way works best for you and makes the most sense to you/for your organization, but just *do it*. Don't do it after you've gotten your pantry up and running for a few months, do it right from the start. Because if you do, you'll be able to say "Wow! When we started this thing 6 months ago, we only fed 7 families and now we are feeding 77!" It's fun (and helpful) to be able to look back over months/years of data and see your progress and trends. So, here's a helpful list of stats to keep:

- Number of Individuals Served Each Day/Month (which means you need to include *dates* in your records!)
- Number of Families Served Each Day/Month
- Pounds of Food Given Away
- New Families Who Shop Each Month
- Consistent Families Who Shop Each Month
- Number of Businesses Donating to Your Cause
- Number of Individuals Donating to Your Cause
- Number of People Eating in Your Soup Kitchen Each Day/Month
- Average Age of People Who Shop

There are plenty of other stats categories you can keep. It's unique to each organization. I don't care *what* stats you keep, just make sure you keep some! And share them with your donors.

Taxes

Taxes are tricky. Especially for nonprofit organizations. I learned the hard way that taxes suck when you are in charge of an organization. I want you to start out the *easy* way and never have a problem! Although, we're talking about the IRS here, so "never having a problem" is not really all that likely…my goal, then, is to at least make sure that you don't make the big mistakes that most nonprofits do and to give you the tools to equip you to make the IRS happy so they'll leave you alone! Let's face it: you have enough on your plate without having to add some personality-filled (sarcasm) IRS agent calling and emailing you every day, right? Right. Let's avoid that at all costs. Here we go.

Important Factoid #1: The form you will probably use for filing your taxes is Form 990 or Form 990EZ. You can find a PDF for both online.

Important Factoid #2: KNOW YOUR FISCAL YEAR END DATE. Pick a date and write it down. It's easiest to make December 31st your fiscal year end date. The IRS has special rules for when nonprofits file their taxes, but you HAVE to keep a consistent fiscal year end date. Even if you start your organization in November, I would still pick December 31st as your fiscal year end. We tried to make ours in the middle of the year and it just got all screwed up. The IRS website says:

"File Form 990 by the 15th day of the 5th month after the organization's accounting period ends (May 15th for a calendar-year filer). If the regular due date falls on a Saturday, Sunday, or legal holiday, file on the next business day. A business day is any day that is not a Saturday, Sunday, or legal holiday."

So, if your "accounting period" ends on December 31st, your taxes are due May 15th. **Send them early.** The IRS loves to penalize you for late submission. Don't let them!! I send ours two months early so that there is **NO WAY** that they can claim that they were late.

Important Factoid #3: Using a professional tax attorney is smart. Can you do it yourself? Yes. But I don't like the pressure, so I hand all of my info off to a professional and let them take care of it. Then all you have to do is sign the completed tax return and they'll even mail it for you! You have to pay them anywhere between $100-400, but it is so worth it.

Important Factoid #4: You can file your taxes electronically. Look into that option. It's called Form 990-N.

Important Factoid #5: There are rules regarding which Form to use when filing:

File Form 990-N if your organization normally has gross receipts of $50,000 or less, it must submit Form 990-N, Electronic Notice (e-Postcard).

File Form 990-EZ if your organization has **gross receipts** less than $200,000 and **total assets** at the end of the tax year less than $500,000, you can file the Short Form Return (Form 990-EZ).

* *File Form 990* if your organization does not meet the requirements to file Form 990-EZ or Form 990-N.

Insurance

Bam. Insurance. Don't we all hate it? Health insurance, vision insurance, dental insurance, home insurance, renter's insurance, liability insurance, J-Lo's rear-end asset insurance, yada yada yada yada. There is insurance for everything. And it feels like sometimes you pay into it for years and then when something actually happens where you *need* the insurance, there is some loophole that doesn't require your insurance company to pay!!!! Okay, stepping down off of my pedestal. Unfortunately, you need to deal with insurance when you run a nonprofit organization, too. And it isn't cheap. If you are operating out of a building of any kind (which, unless you are operating out of a cave or a tent, I will assume a building is part of your efforts), you need coverage for that building in case it burns to the ground or a tornado wipes it out or something else crazy happens. It's better to be insured than not. Simple as that. If you use vehicles to transport food, insure them. If you have employees, set up Worker's Comp insurance. If you have a Board of Directors, get insurance to protect them, too. You need it all. Any Joe Blow could walk in to your pantry, get his big boy panties all up in a twist for some silly reason and then file some crazy lawsuit against you. Somebody could throw their cigarette next to a cardboard box sitting by the pantry, it catches on fire, shoots up to the roof, burns your entire roof down before the fire trucks get there. The likelihood of these things happening? Small. But still. I'd rather be prepared than caught off-guard without insurance! Find an insurance company in your area that can handle all of the various kinds of insurance you need. That way, you have a person you can talk to face-to-face if something comes up.

What Your Food Pantry Should Look Like

I've always been taught and have tried to live by the motto: "If you're going to do something, do it right." Well, it seems to me that successfully feeding *all* of the hungry in your community throughout the year *is* in fact "doing it right". So aim for that. It *is* possible to address, reduce, and even eventually eradicate the hunger problems in our nation. And below, I've summarized the way we have been able to do that successfully in our community.

How To Make Your Pantry Successful

When people hear "food pantry" or "soup kitchen", they usually envision a stuffy church basement open on Mondays and Wednesdays for a few short hours. They picture a large closet with a few shelves and few options. Such a stereotype is the only image brought to mind because it's usually accurate.

Not to disparage the usefulness of the small pantries/kitchens that we've all come to know; for, they *have been* useful and good intentioned. However, just as the "Mom & Pop" grocery stores needed to make way for larger chain stores due to demand, it's time to revamp our idea of food aid/charity in the United States as the need has increased substantially enough to surpass the usefulness of small efforts.

There are several key components that make **Harvesting Hope** (our pantry) both vastly different and more successful in meeting the hunger need in Kentucky. These are the things you want to be true of your pantry if you want it to be successful (and I know you do because you've read this far!):

1. **Convenient**: Both our food pantry and our soup kitchen are open 5 days a week. This allows for everyone – regardless of work schedule, transportation issues, etc. – to find a time and day to make it to the pantry/kitchen to get aid. If you can swing it, have *your* pantry be open 7 days a week!

2. Combined: How often do you find a food pantry *and* a soup kitchen paired together in one location? This allows us to provide a warm meal *and* groceries to every person who enters our facility in need of food.

3. Comprehensive: We don't merely hand out a few cans of vegetables or soups; we consistently provide a variety of meats, breads, pastries, canned goods, pastas, sweets, both fresh and canned fruits, both fresh and canned vegetables, milk, and many other products to *every* "shopper". We have partnered with God's Food Pantry (Lexington Kentucky's Feeding America affiliate), Wal-Mart, Food Lion, Save-A-Lot, local farmers, and local restaurants to provide us with such a variety (networking *must* be a key component for success). We are virtually a smaller, more condensed, and free grocery store. The image of a free grocery store is a great segue to the fourth difference, which regards the atmosphere of our food pantry;

4. Dignified: We provide shopping carts and shopping bags and allow each shopper to choose which foods he/she goes home with. We feel like this gives people a sense of dignity, respect, and ability (each person feels like he/she is receiving a "hand up" instead of a "hand out", which increases feelings of self-worth and capability to get back on your feet). Don't just hand people a box of food. Let them shop like you and I get to shop for our families. I have included a few examples of how much food we provide for each family in the Forms chapter. Based on family size, there is a certain amount of food that has worked well for us to give.

5. Volunteer Driven: This difference can be summarized in one word: volunteers. We have an abundance of volunteers *every* day. Based on volunteer feedback, the reason they enjoy coming back time and time again is because our environment is fun, friendly, and upbeat versus the usual cold, dreary, disconnected pantries and food charities of the past. Each "shopper" gets a designated volunteer who shops with them, helps load their cart with bags of groceries that the shopper picks, and walks them with their shopping cart to their car and loads their car. Relationships are naturally developed and when you make a connection with the person you are helping, you are more likely to feel invested in the cause for which you are volunteering.

6. Core Staff: There is a core staff of 6 individuals who are paid to run the operation – Executive Director, Co-Director, Volunteer Coordinator, Food Coordinator, Pantry/Kitchen Manager, and Cook. One reason so many good intentioned pantries/kitchens fail to reach their hungry is a lack of funding. Nobody in this economy can dedicate a full-time schedule to any cause for free and expect to be able to provide for *their* family and stay afloat and afire with passion for their work! Hence, the seventh and final significant difference:

7. *Financial support*. You have to spend money to feed people successfully. Refer to the "Money" chapter and work hard to make your pantry financially viable and stable!

Practical Steps for Daily Operation

In this section I'm going to illustrate in steps what it should look like when a new shopper comes in so you can be fully prepared when you open:

Step 1: Hand the shopper a card with a number on it (we have laminated cards with numbers from 1-50. That helps us keep track of who came in first, second, third, etc. and it makes the shopping process smooth) and have them sit down in your waiting area.

Step 2: Get the paperwork ready that you need the shopper to fill out. This includes the intake sheet (sample in Forms section).

Step 3: Call the next number in line and get a copy of their photo ID, social security cards for all individuals living in the home (one person shops for entire household each month), proof of residency (utility bill or something similar; you want to limit your shoppers to only those in your county/area, otherwise you will run out of food way too quickly and you won't be able to help your community the way you intended), and proof of income (I've included the requirements for maximum income in the Forms section; remember that your food pantry is for people in "need" – if you serve people who make above a certain amount required by the state for "income-based need", you are doing a disservice to those who truly need your help). Have them fill out the paperwork.

Step 4: Have the next available volunteer take the food card for that particular shopper's family size (i.e. shopping for 2, shopping for 5, shopping for 7+) and help that shopper shop.

Step 5: The volunteer should help the shopper load their car.

Step 6: Repeat these steps for the next person in line. Depending on how big your shopping space is, you can have anywhere from 1-8 people shopping at the same time with shopping carts and volunteers

While your desk person is going through this process with shoppers, have volunteers be preparing shopping bags/boxes, getting carts ready, stocking shelves, cleaning, talking with waiting shoppers, etc. Always have everybody moving to make your day the most efficient it can be.

If you want to see an example of what all of these steps should look like, simply go to our website at www.harvestinghopeky.org and click on the video link for "Shopper Demonstration" and you can see this process in action.

Closing Remarks

I'm so excited for you. I really hope this small guide has helped you feel better prepared and more motivated to get your food pantry/soup kitchen off the ground (or helped you discover ways to bolster your already up and running organization). It really will make a difference in so many people's lives. I can't even begin to tell you how many times I've had someone say to me or someone on my staff, "I couldn't make it without you guys", "I didn't know how I was going to feed my kids until I heard about you guys," "I've never been treated so kindly before". Running a nonprofit organization isn't a walk in the park by any means (as you've seen by reading through this manual!), but I cannot think of any other job more rewarding. You are literally meeting the basic needs of your neighbors singlehandedly every day. Think about Abraham Maslow's Hierarchy of Needs.

1. *Physiological Needs*: breathing, food, water, shelter, clothing, sleep
2. *Safety and Security*: health, employment, property, family and social stability
3. *Love and Belonging*: friendship, family, intimacy, sense of connection
4. *Self-Esteem*: confidence, achievement, respect of others, the need to be a unique individual
5. *Self-Actualization*: morality, creativity, spontaneity, acceptance, experience purpose, meaning and inner potential

You are meeting at least 4 of those just by feeding people with dignity, love, and respect. You rock. Get your pantry where you want it and then help other people do the same thing! I want this hunger epidemic in our *FIRST WORLD COUNTRY* to be demolished! I have confidence that together we can do it. And do it right. And do it with love. And do it for good. Thanks for joining me in the effort to feed the hungry in our nation! Call me if you need help getting started or if you experience any hang-ups once you've opened your doors! I mean it. Literally. I've included my contact information. Call me. Text me (I'm cool and hip). Email me. Facebook me. Snail mail me. Let's do this.

Forms

Food Waiver
Bylaws
Thank You Letter
End of Year Thank You
Sample Grant Request
Statistics Sheet
Intake Form
Food Cards

Food Donation Waiver

Thank you for your decision to make a food donation to help those in need. The Kentucky State Legislature has decided to encourage such donations by the enactment of Kentucky Revised Statute 413.248. Based upon the Emerson Good Samaritan Food Donation Act, KRS 413.248 eliminates liability to those who donate apparently wholesome food to a nonprofit organization for distribution to the needy. The full text of the Statute is reprinted here in order to keep you informed, and to relieve any concerns you may have:

413.248 Liability of donor for damages resulting from condition of donated food.

(1) A person, including an individual, corporation, partnership, organization, association, or retail food establishment, who donates apparently wholesome food to a nonprofit organization for distribution to the needy is not subject to civil or criminal liability that arises from the condition of the food, unless an injury or death results from an act or omission of the donor which constitutes gross negligence, recklessness, or intentional misconduct.

(2)   A nonprofit organization that distributes apparently wholesome food to the needy at no charge and that substantially complies with applicable local, county, state, and federal laws and regulations regarding the storage and handling of food for distribution to the public is not subject to civil or criminal liability that arises from the condition of the food, unless an injury or death results from an act or omission of the organization that constitutes gross negligence, recklessness, or intentional misconduct.

(3)   This section does not create any liability.

Thank you again for your donation. We hope the above statute will help you feel confident in your decision. We appreciate your good deed and pledge to relieve you of any liability in accordance with the law.

_____

_____

Executive Director

_____   _____

Business Name (Donor)   Date

Harvesting Hope Food Pantry, Inc.

Organization Bylaws

I. Preamble, Name, and Objectives

Section 1. Preamble

Harvesting Hope Food Pantry, Inc. hereby creates this organization for service to the communities in Kentucky that are in need of food assistance. The purpose of the organization is to respond in benevolent action to needs of individuals and families within these communities.

Section 2. Name

The name of this Foundation shall be Harvesting *Hope Food Pantry, Inc.*

Section 3. Objectives

The objective of the *Harvesting Hope Food Pantry, Inc.* shall be:
*To reduce the hunger in Kentucky through community cooperation making the best possible use of all available resources.

II. Board of Directors

Section 1. Composition

The Board of Directors shall be the governing body of *Harvesting Hope Food Pantry, Inc.* , and shall establish policy, direct activities, and approve all actions pertaining to the business of the organization.

The *Harvesting Hope Food Pantry, Inc.* Board of Directors will be made up of no fewer than five Directors and no more than seven Directors.

*The Board of Directors shall have the responsibility to conduct the affairs of the organization in a prudent manner in accordance with its bylaws.

*The Board of Directors shall approve and authorize the official acts of the elected or appointed officers

*The Board of Directors shall be responsible for identifying needs to be responded to by the organization.

Section 2. Term of Office

The term of office for the *Harvesting Hope Food Pantry, Inc.* Board of Directors shall be two years, and may be reappointed for successive terms. The initial Board of Directors will be appointed by members of the Hand Up Group.

A Board member can be removed from office for conduct that does not reflect the spirit and objectives of the organization. The remove a Board member requires a unanimous vote of the Executive Committee and a two-thirds (2/3) vote of all Board members.

Section 3. Election of Officers

The Officers of the organization shall be a Chairperson, a Treasurer, and a Secretary. The initial appointment of these officers shall be by members of the Hand Up Group and may be reappointed on an annual basis. The Officers will serve as the Executive Committee of the Board of Directors.

Section 4. Executive Committee

The Executive Committee of the Board of Directors shall consist of the Officers of the organization. The Executive Committee shall be empowered to act for the Board of Directors between meetings of the Board of Directors. All activities of the Executive Committee will be reported in writing at the next scheduled meeting of the Board of Directors.

III. Meetings of the Board of Directors

Section 1. Meetings

The *Harvesting Hope Food Pantry, Inc.* Board of Directors will meet at least quarterly, subject to the call of the Chairperson.

Section 2. Quorum

A quorum shall consist of fifty-one percent of Directors present. There shall be no proxy voting.

IV. Amendments

These bylaws may be amended by a two-thirds (2/3) vote of the Board of Directors, provided the amendment has been submitted in writing at least thirty (30) days prior to a scheduled meeting of the Board of Directors.

Thank You Letter

We just wanted to take the time to say thank you for your tax-deductible donation of _____ Every penny you donated is precious to us and will help put food on the tables of families that are hungry and in desperate need to feel as though someone cares; for, everyone deserves the dignity of being able to provide food for themselves and their families.

With the help of people like you, we are able to feed over **2,000** people a month between our food pantry and soup kitchen and, to date, we have fed over **2,200** households! That's over **2,200** **families** who are now able to go to bed with full stomachs instead of with that growling reminder of the rough patch in life that they currently have found themselves in. Your contribution alone will provide _____ meals to hungry people in Boyle County!

Because of you, we get to see smiles and hope on faces where there was once fear and uncertainty. Thank you for joining with us to reduce the hunger in Boyle County and to meet the needs of our neighbors.

May God bless you as you have been a blessing to others,

Amber W. Sellars, Director
&
The Harvesting Hope Staff

"To whom much is given, much is required." – Luke 12:48

End Of Year Thank You Letter

Harvesting Hope Food Pantry, Inc.
EIN: 27-3158225

Name: _____

Tax-Deductible Donation Total for 2012: $_____

Thank you for your contributions. Because of you and others like you, in 2012 we were able to:

- feed 2,211 unique hungry families in Boyle County this year (556 of those families were **new** families this year)
- serve between 1,200-1,700 people *every month*
- hand out groceries 7,027 times
- serve 8,298 meals in the soup kitchen

Statistically, these numbers suggest that we were able to feed every hungry person in Boyle County at least once this year (many of those people every day this year!). That is absolutely incredible.

Our fundraising goal this year to feed Boyle County was $100,000. With your donation(s) included, we raised $108,579.05! Our fundraising goal for 2013 is $200,000 so that we can mobilize our efforts and feed those in Boyle County who cannot physically get to the pantry and soup kitchen. We are also taking what we've done here and helping other counties get a Harvesting Hope Food Pantry & Soup Kitchen started for *their* neighbors!

We could not have done and cannot do any of this without your help. And we truly believe that, together, we can eliminate the hunger problem here in Boyle County and eventually in the rest of Kentucky. Please consider supporting us in 2013. You have been a tremendous blessing and we cannot thank you enough. Please let us know if the above donation totals are incorrect in any way.

Authorized Representative's Signature:

_____   _____

Amber W. Sellars, Executive Director   Date

Sample Grant Request

March 14, 2012

Dear Grants Officer,

Harvesting Hope Food Pantry, Inc. seeks $20,000 to help us move toward serving more hungry people in our county. The Harvesting Hope Food Pantry – which opened in July 2010 - is a 501(c)(3) non-profit organization who's mission is to reduce the hunger in Boyle County through *community* cooperation making the best possible use of all available resources. We strive to make the operation of our pantry a community effort. We run the pantry almost completely on volunteer availability and dedication. We want our community to be united in the effort to better the lives of our neighbors by meeting their basic needs. Although we definitely need and would benefit from outside monetary resources, our greatest desire is to eventually get to a place in our county where our pantry is completely self sustained by our community – individuals, businesses, organizations, etc. Initial grant funds in these early years of our development would be a huge aid in getting us to that place.

Our passion for feeding the hungry in our community stems from the overwhelming poverty statistics in our state to date. Kentucky is the seventh poorest state in the nation. Right now, nearly *820,140* people in our state are living in poverty and are at risk for hunger. In Boyle County alone, there are roughly *5,200* people living under the poverty level who are in desperate need of food. They are people we meet and interact with every day – the person driving your child's school bus each day, the lady who cuts your hair, the sweet retired couple who sit behind you at church. Hunger does not discriminate. Devastatingly, children and seniors are disproportionately affected by hunger and more than 60% of households served include either a child or a senior citizen. Each month, our pantry feeds over 1,600 of those people with donations from community businesses and members. With a population of just over *29,000* (18% at risk for hunger) people in our community, Harvesting Hope is reaching nearly *1 in 3.25* (*30%*) hungry people each month. We are happy to be meeting the need for that 30%, but we want to reach the other 70%!

Our goal is to get to a place financially where we can feed as close to the 18% in need in our community as possible. We would like to reach this goal in the next two years. One of the ways we can accomplish this is through fundraising efforts (both from grant providers and from fundraising in the community), which we are currently working on vigorously. Our current monthly operations budget - including rent, utilities, personnel costs, and food costs - is roughly $18,000, which provides food for the aforementioned 1,600 people in our community. We are seeking funding in the amount of $20,000 to help us move toward serving more people in our county. It costs us only $0.19 per pound to purchase food. With $20,000, we could purchase 105,263 pounds of food which would provide approximately 90,000 meals to those in need in our community (for every $10 we receive, we are able to provide roughly 45 meals to people in need). We keep diligent track of the number of individuals and families that we serve at the pantry each month. We also keep track of the amount of food (quantities and pounds) we receive. Therefore, we will be able to measure the beneficial outcome of any monies we receive through grants easily, simply by calculating the number of individuals and families served and the quantities and pounds of food received with the use of the grant money.

Thank you for taking the time to consider our proposal. With your help, we can reduce the staggering amount of hunger that is plaguing so many innocent members of our community. Food is a basic need and we feel fortunate and blessed to have the opportunity to meet that need for the thousands of our neighbors who are looking to us for help. We believe that any money we receive will work to support what we believe in - to change lives and make our community a better place. If you have any questions, please do not hesitate to call or email us at (859) 583-7811 or awsellars@me.com.

Sincerely,

Amber W. Sellars, Executive Director

Statistics Sheet

_____ *(Month, Year)*

Date	Last Month → New Families	Last Month → Total Families	Last Month → Total Individuals
-			
-			
-			
-			
-			
-			
-			
-			
-			
-			
-			
-			
-			
-			
-			
-			
-			
-			
-			
-			
-			
-			
-			
-			
-			
-			

TOTALS

Pounds of Food Donated:_____

Food Card Examples

Family of 1

Category	Amount
Frozen Meats	1
Eggs	1 dozen
Fresh produce	6
Sweets	4
Bread	2
Peanutbutter/Beans	2 jars/cans/packages
Canned Meat	1 cans
Pasta/Flour/Rice/Cereal	5
Canned Veg/Fruit/Soup	6 cans
Formula	2 cans
Baby Food	10 jars
Extras	6

Family of 7+

Category	Amount
Frozen Meats	1
Eggs	1 dozen
Fresh produce	6
Sweets	4
Bread	2
Peanutbutter/Beans	4 jars/cans/packages
Canned Meat	3 cans
Pasta/Flour/Rice/Cereal	8
Canned Veg/Fruit/Soup	12 cans
Formula	2 cans
Baby Food	10 jars
Extras	8

Intake Form

HARVESTING
H♥PE
Food Pantry

Applicant's Name _____
Birth Date _____
Address

_____
Number in Household_____

DATE	CLIENT SIGNATURE

Income eligibility guidelines for USDA Commodities

Household Size	Monthly Income
1	$1,723
2	$2,333
3	$2,944
4	$3,554
5	$4,165
6	$4,775
7	$5,386
8	$5,996

Each Additional Family Member $+611

APPLICANT: PLEASE READ

I certify that my monthly gross household income is at or below the guidelines on the left based on the number of persons in my household. I also certify that, as of today, my household resides in the geographic area served by this Kentucky Emergency Food Assistance Program agency as determined by the administering Food Bank and that I have not previously participated in the Program this month. This form is being completed in connection with the receipt of Federal assistance. I understand that making false certification may result in having to pay the State for the value of the food improperly used to me and may subject me to criminal prosecution under

www.ingramcontent.com/pod-product-compliance
Lightning Source LLC
Chambersburg PA
CBHW052109270326
41931CB00012B/2945